Capetown Ambush
DONALD BROWN

Recorded by DONALD BROWN on SOURCES OF INSPIRATION
Muse: MCD 5385 (CD)

EDDIE HENDERSON, trumpet
GARY BARTZ, soprano sax
DONALD BROWN, piano
BUSTER WILLIAMS, bass
CARL ALLEN, drums

Recorded on August 11, 1989

QUINTET INSTRUMENTATION
(recorded parts shown in bold type, alternate parts in light type)
1st part: **Trumpet**, Alto Sax, C♭
2nd part: **Soprano Sax**, Alto Sax, Trombone
Rhythm Section: **Piano, Bass, Drums**, Guitar
FULL SCORE

Recorded by DONALD BROWN on SOURCES OF INSPIRA... (J-5385)
FULL SCORE
Capetown Am...
DONALD BROWN
Latin (♩ = ca. 224)
Intro
Trumpet
Soprano Sax
Intro
Piano
mf
Bass
Drums
Tpt
Sop
Pno
Bass
Dr
engraved by Osho Endo

Capetown Ambush

Capetown Ambush

Tpt
Sop
Pno
Bass
Dr
29
mp
mp
mp
Tpt
Sop
Pno
Bass
Dr
33

Tpt
Sop
Pno
Bass
Dr
mf
mf
mf
mp
f
f
f
f
37
solo fills
41
Capetown Ambush

Tpt
Sop
Pno
Bass
Dr
solo fills
45
Tpt
Sop
Pno
Bass
Dr
solo fills
49

Tpt
Sop
Pno
Bass
Dr
53
C
57
Capetown Ambush

Tpt
Sop
Pno
Bass
Dr
simile
pedal ad lib.
simile
61
65
Capetown Ambush

* The Piano solos first on the recording, accompanied only by Drums. After the Bass enters,
further strengthening the Bb pedal, the horns enter in a dialog as the energy increases to a high point,
after which the intensity diminishes *(D.S. al fine)*.

Recorded by DONALD BROWN on SOURCES OF INSPIRATION (Muse MCD-5385)
RECORDED
TRUMPET (1st part)
Capetown Ambush
DONALD BROWN
Latin (♩ = ca. 224)
Intro
8
11
Piano
Piano and Drums
mf
A
21
25
29
33
mp
1.
2.
37
mf
f
B
41
Copyright © 1990 SECOND FLOOR MUSIC
This arrangement copyright © 1991 SECOND FLOOR MUSIC
International Copyright Secured   All Rights Reserved   Made in U.S.A.
engraved by Osho Endo

* The Piano solos first on the recording, accompanied only by Drums. After the Bass enters,
   further strengthening the C pedal, the horns enter in a dialog as the energy increases to a high point,
   after which the intensity diminishes *(D.S. al fine)*.

Capetown Ambush

engraved by Osho Endo

* The Piano solos first on the recording, accompanied only by Drums. After the Bass enters,
  further strengthening the G pedal, the horns enter in a dialog as the energy increases to a high point,
  after which the intensity diminishes (D.S. al fine).

Capetown Ambush

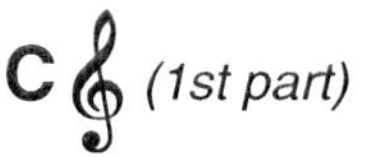

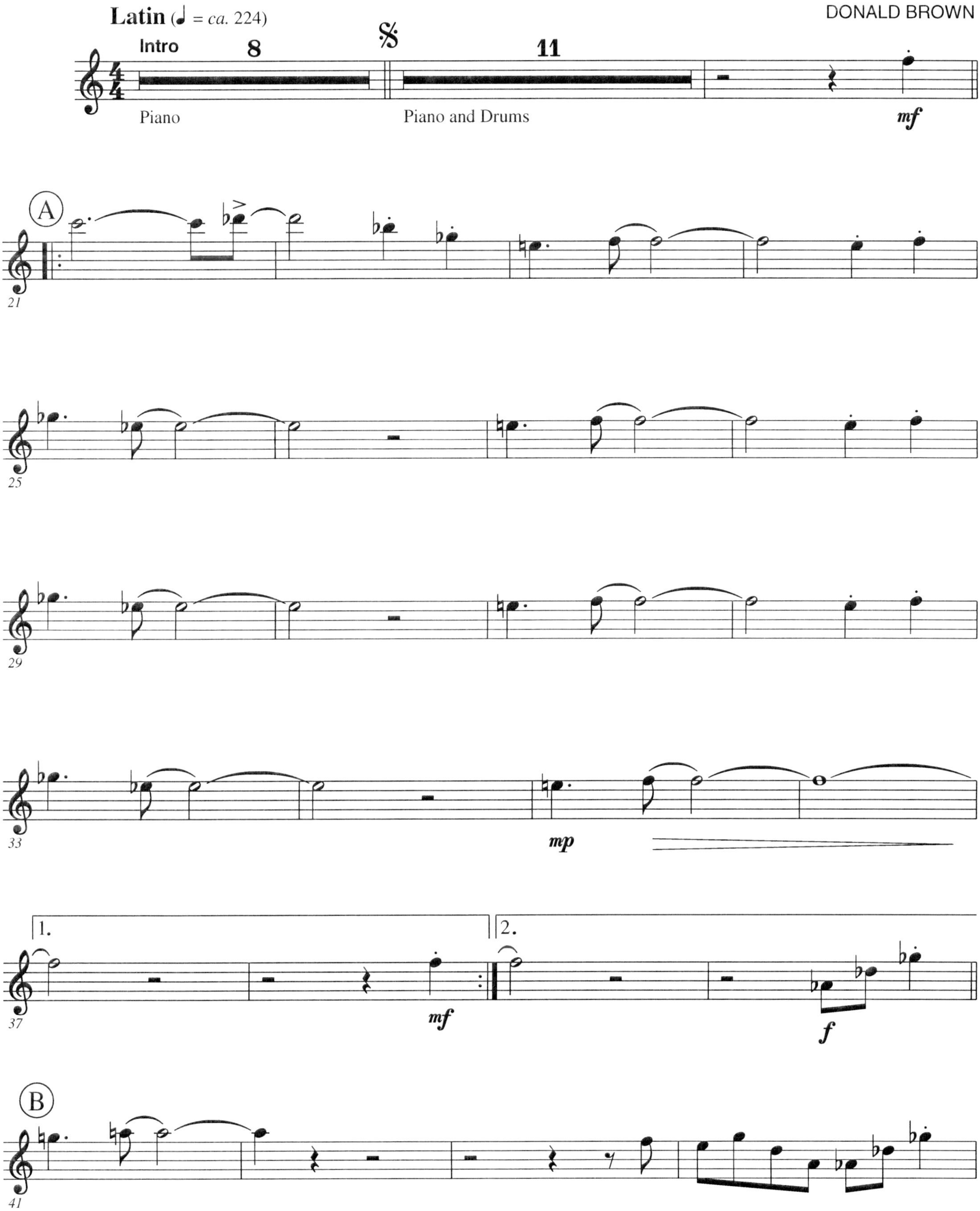

* The Piano solos first on the recording, accompanied only by Drums. After the Bass enters,
   further strengthening the Bb pedal, the horns enter in a dialog as the energy increases to a high point,
   after which the intensity diminishes *(D.S. al fine).*

Capetown Ambush

* The Piano solos first on the recording, accompanied only by Drums. After the Bass enters,
  further strengthening the C pedal, the horns enter in a dialog as the energy increases to a high point,
  after which the intensity diminishes (D.S. al fine).

Recorded by DONALD BROWN on SOURCES OF INSPIRATION (Muse MCD-5385)
Capetown Ambush
ALTO SAX (2nd part)
DONALD BROWN
Latin (♩ = ca. 224)
Intro
Piano
Piano and Drums
mf
A
mf
mp
1.
mf
2.
f
B
f
Copyright © 1990 SECOND FLOOR MUSIC
This arrangement copyright © 1991 SECOND FLOOR MUSIC
International Copyright Secured   All Rights Reserved   Made in U.S.A.
engraved by Osho Endo

* The Piano solos first on the recording, accompanied only by Drums. After the Bass enters,
  further strengthening the G pedal, the horns enter in a dialog as the energy increases to a high point,
  after which the intensity diminishes *(D.S. al fine)*.

Recorded by DONALD BROWN on SOURCES OF INSPIRATION (Muse MCD-5385)
Capetown Ambush
TROMBONE (2nd part)
DONALD BROWN
Latin (♩ = ca. 224)
Intro
8
11
Piano
Piano and Drums
mf
A
21
25
29
33
mp
1.
2.
37
mf
f
B
opt. 8va
41
Copyright © 1990 SECOND FLOOR MUSIC
This arrangement copyright © 1991 SECOND FLOOR MUSIC
International Copyright Secured   All Rights Reserved   Made in U.S.A.
engraved by Osho Endo

* The Piano solos first on the recording, accompanied only by Drums. After the Bass enters,
   further strengthening the Bb pedal, the horns enter in a dialog as the energy increases to a high point,
   after which the intensity diminishes *(D.S. al fine)*.

Capetown Ambush

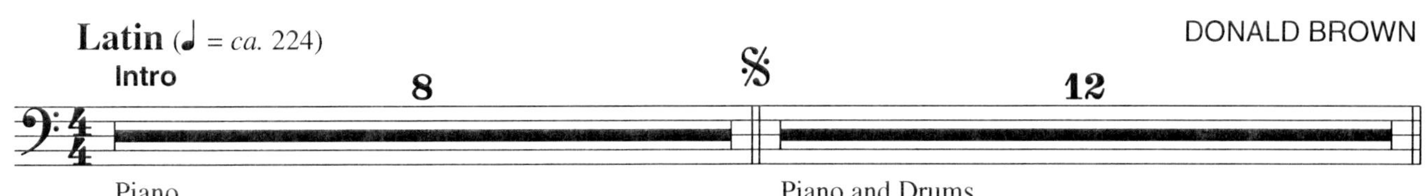

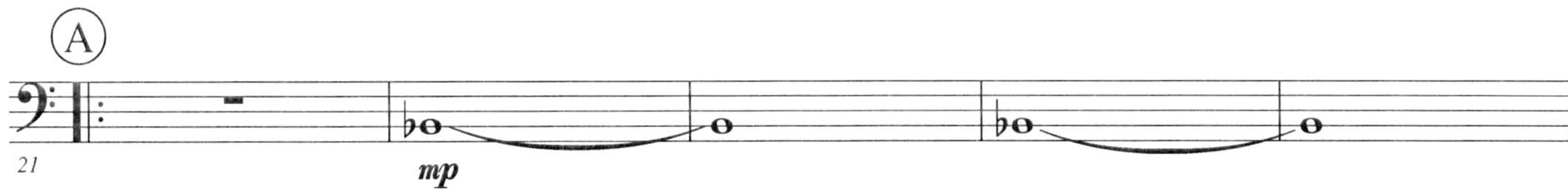

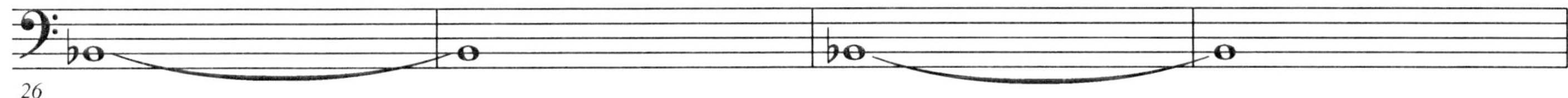

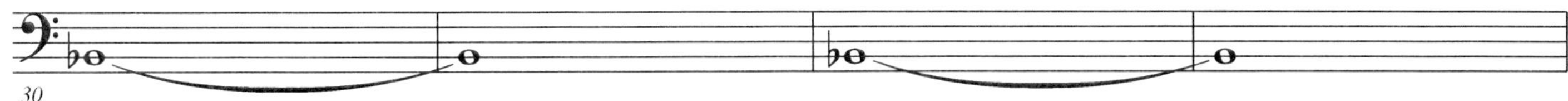

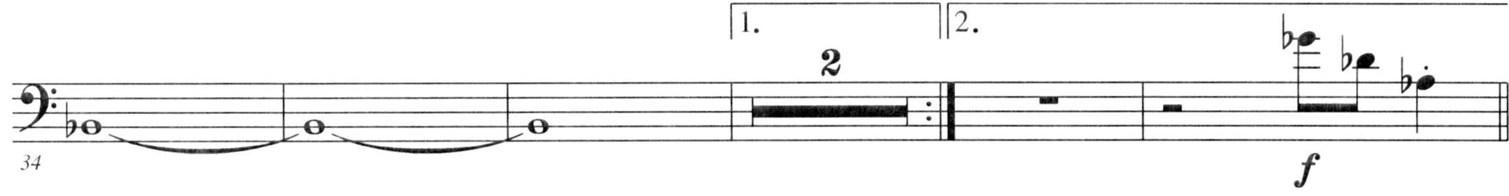

engraved by Osho Endo

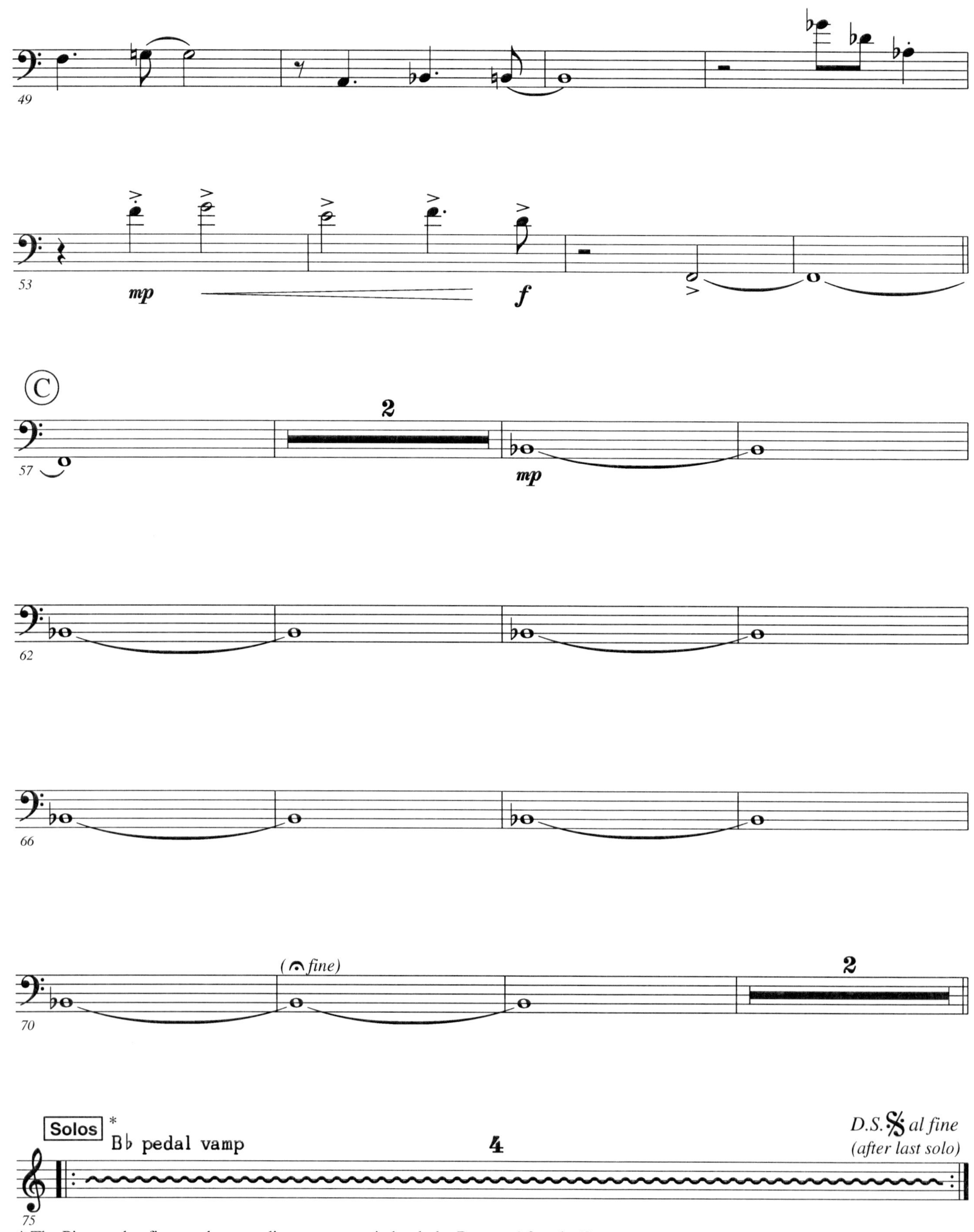

* The Piano solos first on the recording, accompanied only by Drums. After the Bass enters,
further strengthening the B♭ pedal, the horns enter in a dialog as the energy increases to a high point,
after which the intensity diminishes *(D.S. al fine)*.

Recorded by DONALD BROWN on SOURCES OF INSPIRATION (Muse MCD-5385)

Capetown Ambush

DONALD BROWN

Copyright © 1990 SECOND FLOOR MUSIC
This arrangement copyright © 1991 SECOND FLOOR MUSIC
International Copyright Secured   All Rights Reserved   Made in U.S.A.

engraved by Osho Endo

* The Piano solos first on the recording, accompanied only by Drums. After the Bass enters,
  further strengthening the B♭ pedal, the horns enter in a dialog as the energy increases to a high point,
  after which the intensity diminishes(*D.S. al fine*).

Recorded by DONALD BROWN on SOURCES OF INSPIRATION (Muse MCD-5385)
GUITAR (rhythm section)
Capetown Ambush
DONALD BROWN
Latin (= ca. 224)
Intro
simile
A
mf
mp
1.
2.
f

* The Piano solos first on the recording, accompanied only by Drums. After the Bass enters,
  further strengthening the Bb pedal, the horns enter in a dialog as the energy increases to a high point,
  after which the intensity diminishes *(D.S. 𝄋 al fine)*.

Capetown Ambush

DONALD BROWN

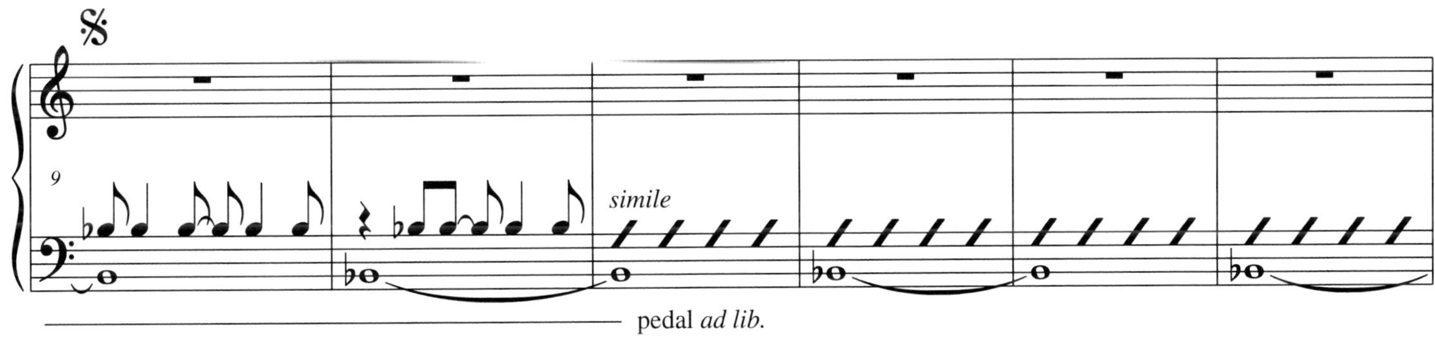

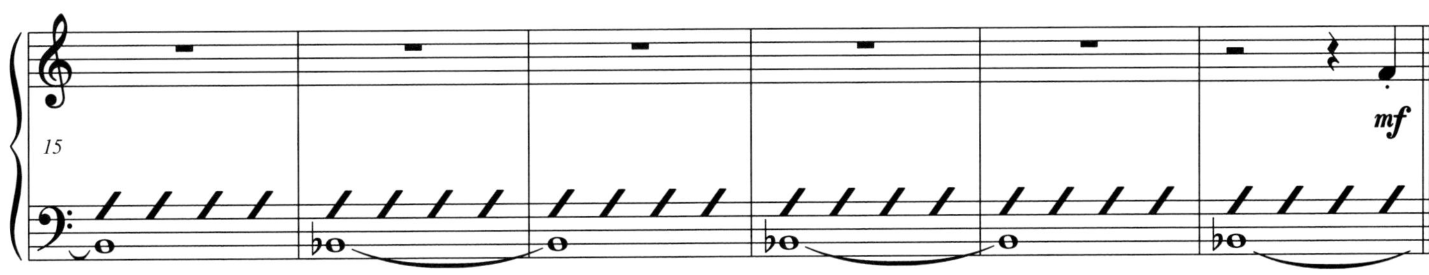

engraved by Osho Endo

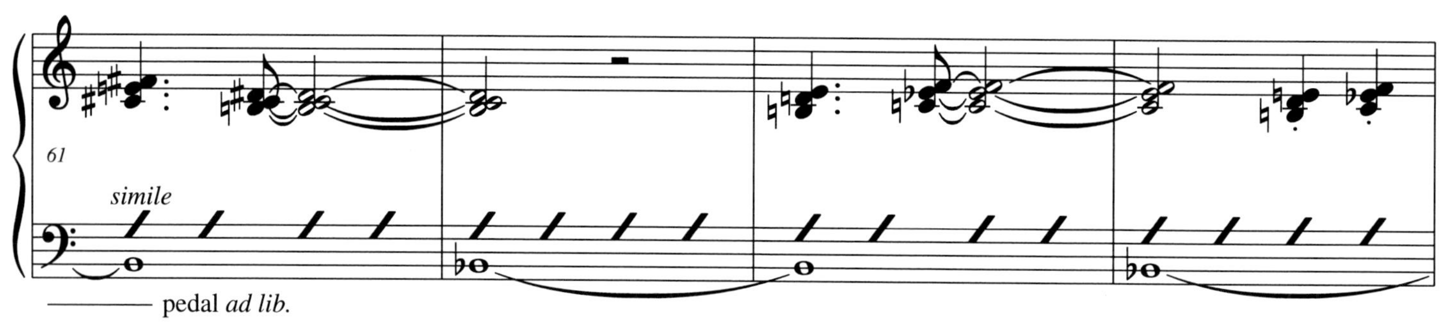

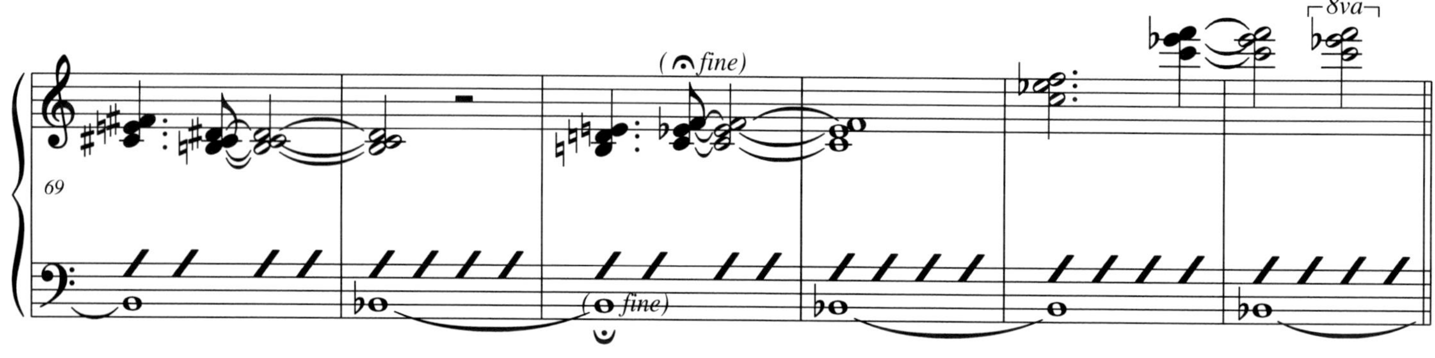

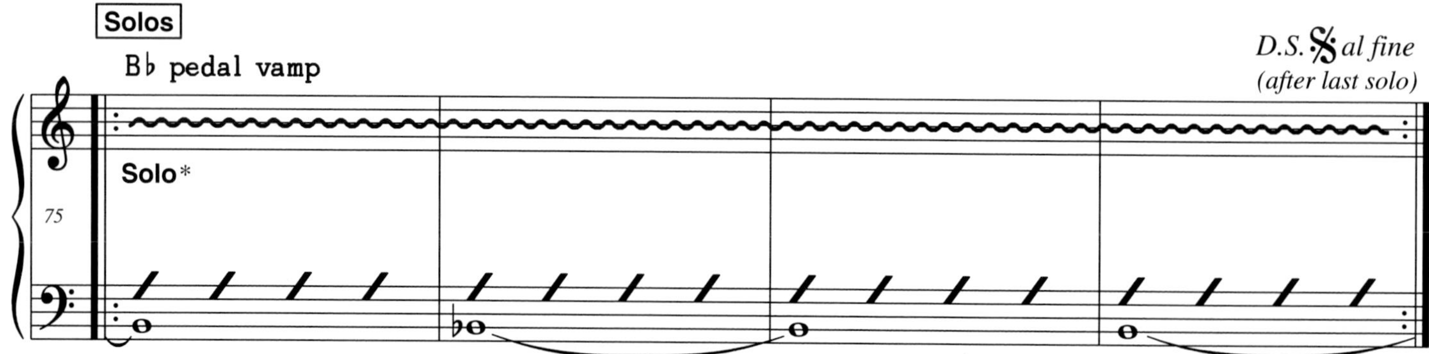

* The Piano solos first on the recording, accompanied only by Drums. After the Bass enters,
further strengthening the Bb pedal, the horns enter in a dialog as the energy increases to a high point,
after which the intensity diminishes *(D.S. 𝄋 al fine)*.

B
41
45
49
53
mp
f
mp
C
57
mf
p

* No bass note in meas. 21 on repeat.